Success With
Writing

■SCHOLASTIC

Editor: Ourania Papacharalambous
Cover design by Tannaz Fassihi; cover illustration by Kevin Zimmer
Interior design by Cynthia Ng
Interior illustrations by Roger Simó (7, 9–10, 15–20, 22–23, 25, 28, 33–35, 40–43, 45); Doug Jones (spot art)
All other images © Shutterstock.com

ISBN 978-1-338-79870-8
Scholastic Inc., 557 Broadway, New York, NY 10012
Copyright © 2022 Scholastic Inc.
All rights reserved. Printed in the U.S.A.
First printing, January 2022
2 3 4 5 6 7 8 9 10   40   29 28 27 26 25 24

INTRODUCTION

One of the greatest challenges teachers and parents face is helping children develop independent writing skills. Each writing experience is unique and individualized. The high-interest topics and engaging exercises in *Scholastic Success With Writing* will both stimulate and encourage children as they develop their writing skills. On page 4, you will find a list of the key skills covered in the activities throughout this book. These grade-appropriate skills can be used in daily writing assignments such as journals, stories, and letters to help build confident, independent writers. Like a stepladder, this book will help children reach the next level of independent writing.

TABLE OF CONTENTS

Key Skills 4

That's Amazing! *(Recognize capital letters)* 5

Sweet Dreams! *(Capitalize sentence beginnings)* 6

The Night Sky *(Use periods)* 7

Twinkle, Twinkle, Little Star *(Punctuate statements)* 8

Hop to It! *(Capitalize/Punctuate statements)* 9

Hop to It Some More!
(Capitalize/Punctuate statements) 10

Striped Sentences *(Identify a sentence)* 11

High-Flying Sentences *(Identify a sentence)* 12

At the Seashore *(Sequence a sentence)* 13

In the Rain Forest *(Sequence a sentence)* 14

Snakes Alive!
(Parts of a sentence: Naming part) 15

Slithering Sentences
(Parts of a sentence: Naming part) 16

Who Is That? *(Parts of a sentence: Naming part)* 17

Where Is That?
(Parts of a sentence: Naming part) 18

Vacation Photos *(Write a sentence)* 19

More Vacation Photos *(Write a sentence)* 20

No Bones About It!
(Parts of a sentence: Identify the action) 21

Mighty Good Sentences
(Parts of a sentence: Complete the action) 22

A Busy Classroom
(Parts of a sentence: Write the verb) 23

Pencil It In
(Parts of a sentence: Determine the verb) 24

Topsy-Turvy! *(Write sentences)* 25

What Is Going On? *(Write sentences)* 26

The Caboose *(Understand sentence parts)* 27

When Was That? *(Identify sentence parts)* 28

Chugging Along *(Understand sentence parts)* 29

My Busy Day *(Complete a sentence)* 30

Silly Sentences *(Write 3-part sentences)* 31

Sweet Sentences *(Write 3-part sentences)* 32

Home Sweet Home *(Write 3-part sentences)* 33

The Construction Crew
(Write 3-part sentences) 34

Mystery Boxes *(Explore adjectives)* 35

Sensational Words *(Add adjectives)* 36

More Describing Words *(Adjectives)* 37

Pretty Packages *(Brainstorm adjectives)* 38

What's Inside?
(Complete describing sentences) 39

Around Town *(Write descriptive sentences)* 40

Keep It in Order *(Complete a sequenced story)* 41

What's Next? *(Write sequenced directions)* 42

Which Title Fits? *(Name a story)* 43

A Terrific Title *(Parts of a story: Write the title)* 44

Story Strips *(Parts of a story:*
Write the beginning, middle, and end) 45

More Story Strips
(Parts of a story: Retell a 3-part story) 46

Answer Key 47

Grade-Appropriate Skills Covered in
Scholastic Success With Writing: Grade 1

Know and use various text features to locate key facts or information in a text.

Demonstrate understanding of the organization and basic features of print.

Recognize the distinguishing features of a sentence.

Know and apply grade-level phonics and word analysis skills in decoding words.

Read words with inflectional endings.

Recognize and read grade-appropriate irregularly spelled words.

Write informative/explanatory texts that name a topic, supply some facts about the topic, and provide some sense of closure.

Write narratives that recount two or more appropriately sequenced events, include some details regarding what happened, use temporal words to signal event order, and provide some sense of closure.

Demonstrate command of the conventions of standard English grammar and usage when writing or speaking.

Print all upper- and lowercase letters.

Use common, proper, and possessive nouns.

Use singular and plural nouns with matching verbs in basic sentences.

Use personal, possessive, and indefinite pronouns.

Use verbs to convey a sense of past, present, and future.

Use frequently occurring adjectives.

Use frequently occurring conjunctions.

Use determiners.

Use frequently occurring prepositions.

Produce and expand complete simple and compound declarative, interrogative, imperative, and exclamatory sentences in response to prompts.

Demonstrate command of the conventions of standard English capitalization, punctuation, and spelling when writing.

Capitalize dates and names of people.

Use end punctuation for sentences.

Use commas in dates and to separate single words in a series.

Use conventional spelling for words with common spelling patterns and for frequently occurring irregular words.

That's Amazing!

Help the mouse through the maze by coloring each box with a word that begins with a capital letter.

A sentence begins with a **capital letter**.

The	For	That	with	know	but
here	on	When	Have	next	we
as	after	good	Make	there	see
Go	Look	Are	Could	is	why
This	who	said	in	come	them
Has	Name	Before	Her	Where	The

 Read the back of a cereal box. How many capital letters did you find? Write the number next to the cheese.

Sweet Dreams!

Write each beginning correctly to make a sentence.

1 my dog _____

_____ runs in her sleep.

2 she must _____

_____ be dreaming.

3 maybe she _____

_____ is chasing a cat.

4 sometimes she _____

_____ even barks.

5 i think _____

_____ it is funny.

 On another sheet of paper, write a sentence about a dream you remember. Circle the capital letter at the beginning of your sentence.

The Night Sky

Add a period to each sentence.

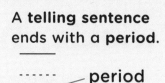

1. Many things shine in the sky at night__

2. The moon looks the brightest__

3. It is closest to Earth__

4. The stars look like tiny dots__

5. They are very far away__

6. The sun is a star__

7. Planets look like colored stars__

8. Their light does not twinkle__

9. Shooting stars look like stars that are falling__

10. There are many things to see in the night sky__

Twinkle, Twinkle, Little Star

Rewrite each sentence using periods.

1 Tonight I saw a star

2 I saw the star twinkle

3 It looked like a candle

4 It was very bright

5 I made a wish

6 I hope it comes true

Hop to It!

Rewrite each sentence correctly.

A **telling sentence** begins with a **capital letter** and ends with a **period**.

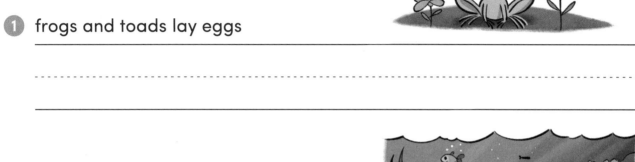

1 frogs and toads lay eggs

2 the eggs are in the water

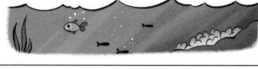

3 tadpoles hatch from the eggs

4 the tadpoles grow legs

5 the tadpoles lose their tails

Hop to It Some More!

Rewrite each sentence correctly.

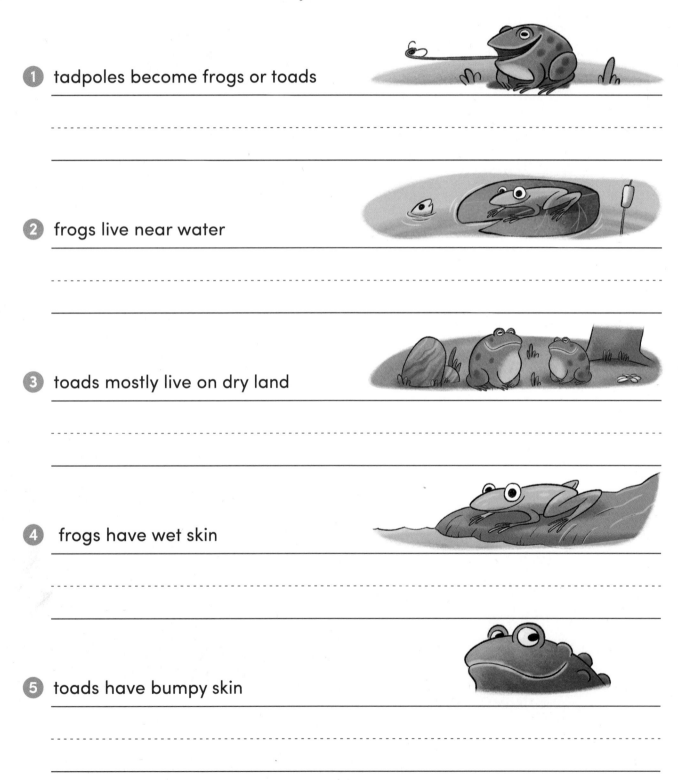

1 tadpoles become frogs or toads

_____

- -

_____

2 frogs live near water

_____

- -

_____

3 toads mostly live on dry land

_____

- -

_____

4 frogs have wet skin

_____

- -

_____

5 toads have bumpy skin

_____

- -

_____

Striped Sentences

A **sentence** tells a complete idea.

Color the rug to show:

GREEN = sentence   **YELLOW** = not a sentence

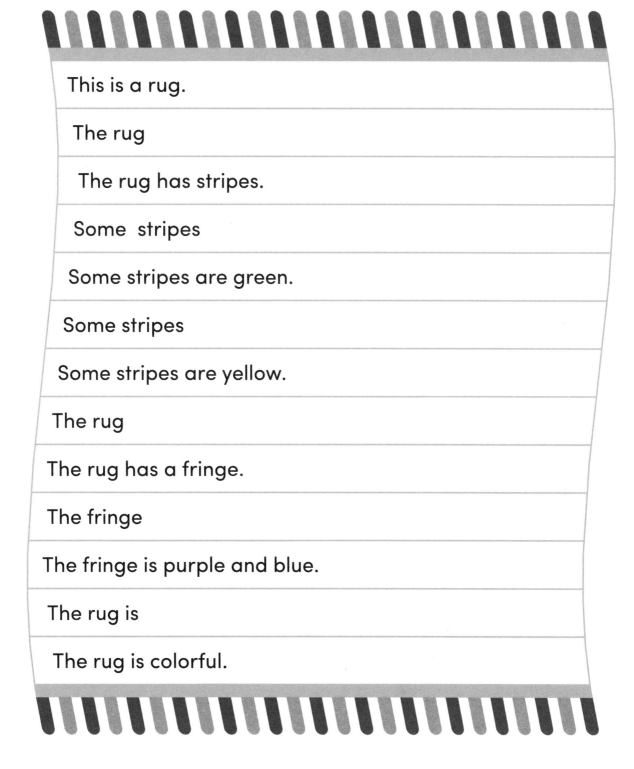

This is a rug.

The rug

The rug has stripes.

Some stripes

Some stripes are green.

Some stripes

Some stripes are yellow.

The rug

The rug has a fringe.

The fringe

The fringe is purple and blue.

The rug is

The rug is colorful.

High-Flying Sentences

Color each flag that tells a complete thought. Leave the other flags blank.

We made a flag.

The big flag

The flag is big.

Blue and purple

It is purple and blue.

I hung it in my room.

In my room

 On another sheet of paper, turn this into a sentence: The biggest flag.

At the Seashore

Unscramble the words to make a sentence.
Write the new sentence below each picture.

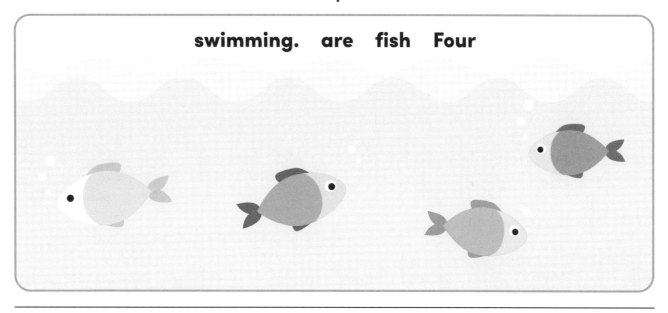

swimming.　are　fish　Four

_____

- -

_____

one　have　We　shovel.

_____

- -

_____

In the Rain Forest

Unscramble the words to make a sentence.
Write the new sentence. Do not forget to put a period at the end.

1 A hiding jaguar is

_____

- -

_____

2 blue Some butterflies are

_____

- -

_____

3 water in jump the Frogs

_____

- -

_____

4 snakes trees Green hang from

_____

- -

_____

5 very tall grow The trees

_____

- -

_____

Scramble a sentence for someone at home.
Be sure the first word begins with a capital letter.

Snakes Alive!

Color the snake that tells the naming part in
each sentence below.

A sentence has a
naming part. It tells
who or what the
sentence is about.

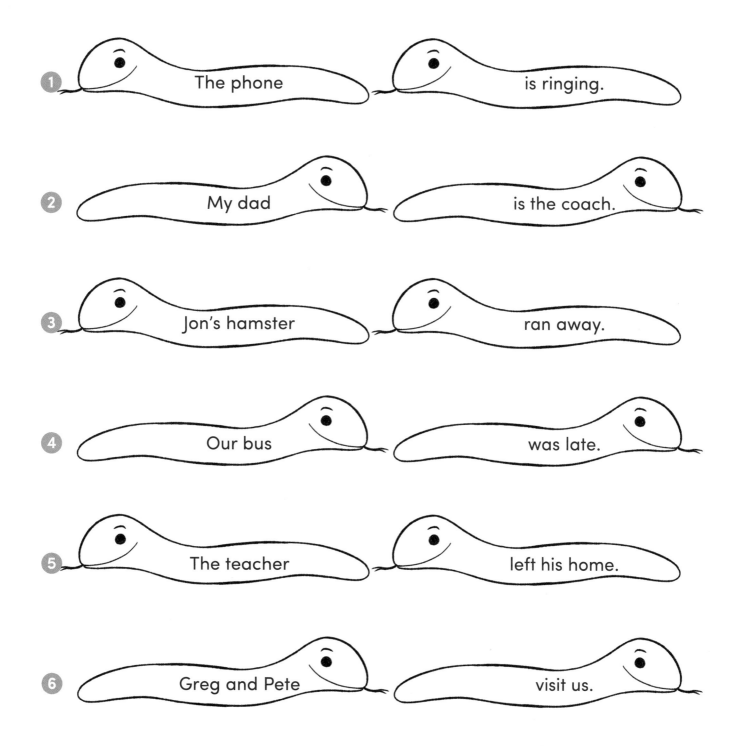

1. The phone — is ringing.

2. My dad — is the coach.

3. Jon's hamster — ran away.

4. Our bus — was late.

5. The teacher — left his home.

6. Greg and Pete — visit us.

Slithering Sentences

Circle the naming part in each sentence below.
Then color the picture to match.

1. The blue snakes are playing.

2. The yellow snake is climbing a tree.

3. The green snake hides under a rock.

4. The brown snake is swimming.

5. The red snake is hanging on a branch.

6. The purple snake sleeps in a tree.

7. The black snake rests on a rock.

8. The orange snake is near an egg.

Who Is That?

Use the pictures to find naming parts to make each sentence complete.

The **naming part** of a sentence can be a person.

1 _____

_____ fell on the ice.

2 _____

_____ ran in the race.

3 _____

_____ went inside the dark cave.

4 _____

_____ climbed the hill.

5 _____

_____ swam across the pool.

Billy

Cam

Luca

Ade

Dario

Where Is That?

Use naming parts to complete each sentence that tells about the map.

Tree Lane

1 _____

_____ is near the swings.

2 _____

_____ is far from the cave.

3 _____

_____ is a good place to fish.

4 _____

_____ has bats inside.

5 _____

_____ is along Tree Lane.

Vacation Photos

Use naming parts to write a complete sentence about each picture.

The **naming part** of a sentence can be a person, place, animal, or thing.

_____

- -

_____

- -

_____

_____

- -

_____

- -

_____

More Vacation Photos

Use naming parts to write a complete sentence about each picture.

_____

- -

_____

- -

_____

_____

- -

_____

- -

_____

No Bones About It!

A sentence has an
action part. It tells
what is happening.

Color the bone that tells the action part in
each sentence below.

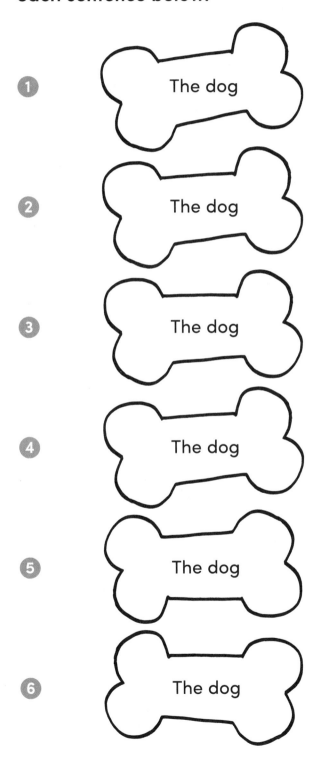
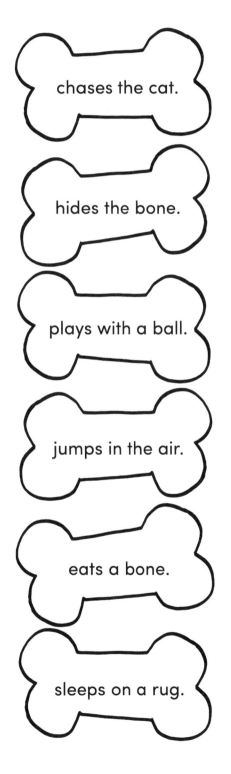

1. The dog — chases the cat.

2. The dog — hides the bone.

3. The dog — plays with a ball.

4. The dog — jumps in the air.

5. The dog — eats a bone.

6. The dog — sleeps on a rug.

Mighty Good Sentences

**Choose the ending that tells what each dog is doing.
Remember to use periods.**

is eating.

is sleeping.

is jumping.

is playing.

1 The white dog _____

_____

2 The gray dog _____

_____

3 The spotted dog _____

_____

4 The striped dog _____

 On another sheet of paper, draw another dog and write a sentence
about it.

A Busy Classroom

The action part of a sentence is called the **verb**.

Complete each sentence with an action verb to tell what is happening in the picture. Remember to use periods.

_____

- -

1 Mr. Downs _____

_____

- -

2 The fish _____

_____

- -

3 James _____

_____

- -

4 Cara _____

Pencil It In

Choose a verb from the Word Bank to complete each sentence.

Sometimes the verb does not show action. It still tells what is happening.

For example:
I **know** the answer.
I **am** hungry.

Word Bank

seems	am	gets	were
is	are	was	eat

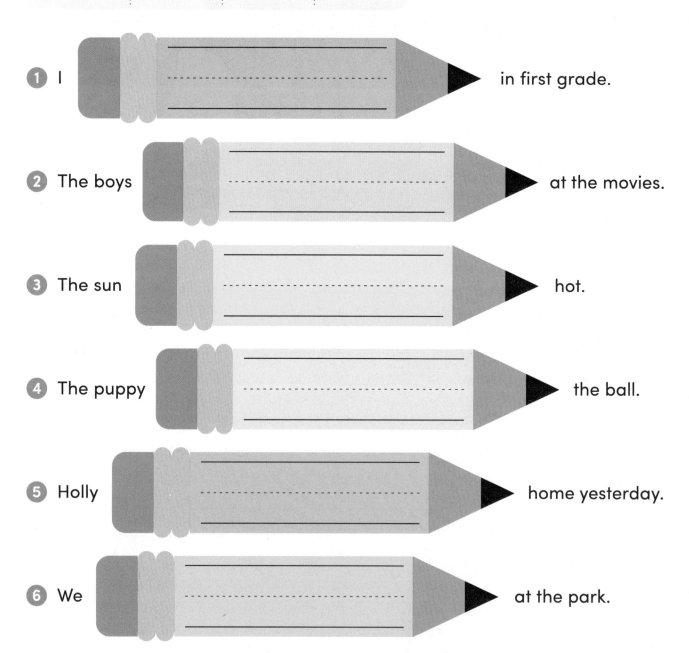

1. I _____ in first grade.

2. The boys _____ at the movies.

3. The sun _____ hot.

4. The puppy _____ the ball.

5. Holly _____ home yesterday.

6. We _____ at the park.

Topsy-Turvy!

Write five sentences that tell what is happening in the pictures.

A sentence has a verb that tells what is happening.

1 _____

2 _____

3 _____

4 _____

5 _____

What Is Going On?

Look around you. Write four sentences that tell what is happening.

1 _____

_____

_____

_____

_____

2 _____

_____

_____

_____

_____

3 _____

_____

_____

_____

_____

4 _____

_____

_____

_____

_____

The Caboose

In each caboose, draw a picture to show where each sentence takes place.

A sentence is more interesting when it tells **where** the action is happening.

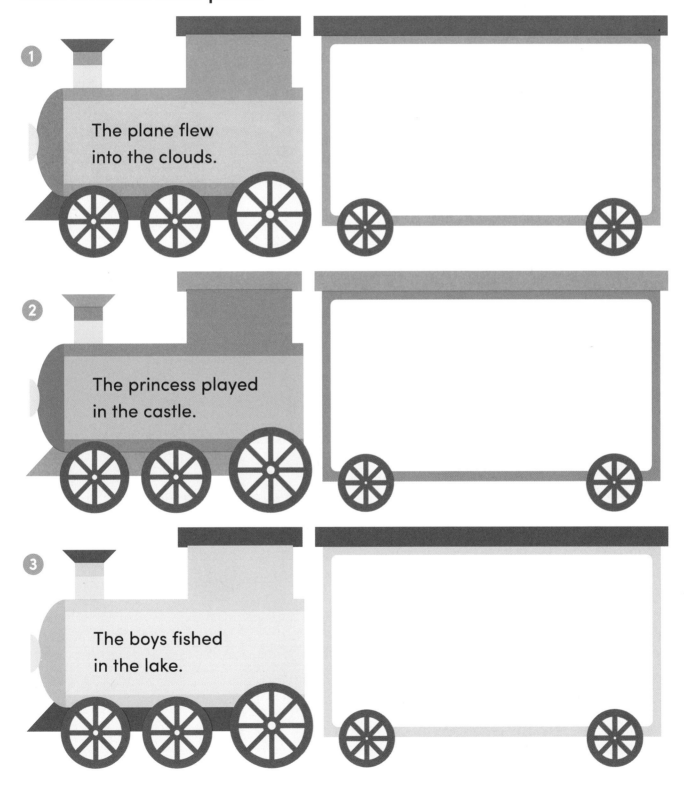

1. The plane flew into the clouds.

2. The princess played in the castle.

3. The boys fished in the lake.

When Was That?

Circle the part that tells when in each sentence.

A sentence may also tell **when** the action takes place.

1. George Washington lived long ago.

2. The mail carrier was late yesterday.

3. The bear slept in winter.

4. We are going to the zoo today.

5. The leaves change in the fall.

6. I lost my tooth last night.

7. It rained all day.

8. The party starts at noon.

9. We got home yesterday.

10. We ate turkey on Thanksgiving Day.

11. The kitten was playing this morning.

12. Tomorrow I am going to my grandmother's house.

Chugging Along

Write an ending for each sentence that tells where
or when the action takes place.

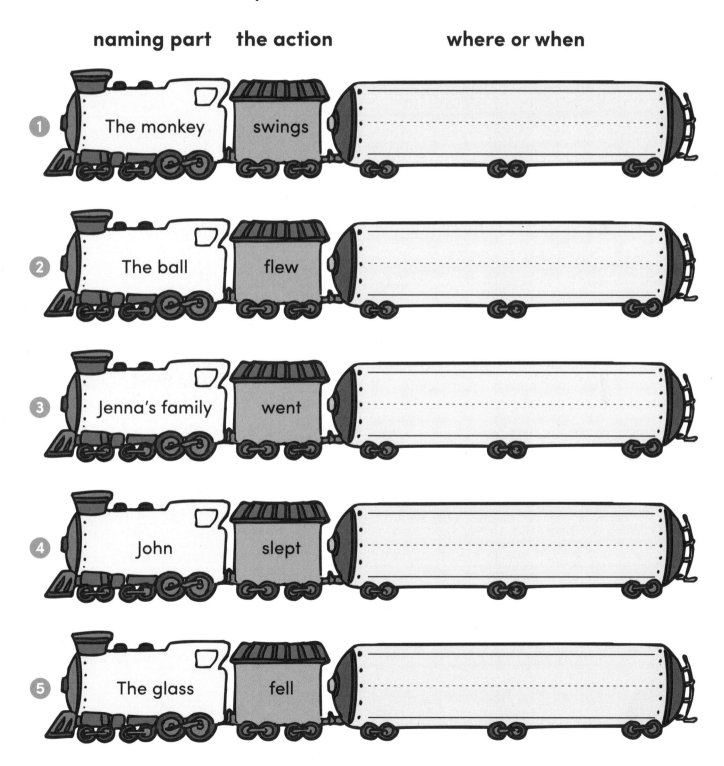

naming part   the action   where or when

1 The monkey   swings

2 The ball   flew

3 Jenna's family   went

4 John   slept

5 The glass   fell

My Busy Day

Write the beginning part of each sentence to tell about your day.
Draw a small picture in the square to match each sentence.

_____

this morning.

_____

this afternoon.

_____

tonight.

 On another sheet of paper, write four sentences and draw four pictures to tell about your best day ever.

Silly Sentences

Complete each missing part to make silly sentences.

A sentence may have three parts: **a naming part, an action,** and a part that tells **where or when.**

the naming part	the action	where or when
1 The monkey		on his head.
2 My dad	is hopping	
3	flipped	in the forest.
4	bounced	on the bed.
5 My shoes		at the pool.
6 The snake	twisted	
7 The bubbles	filled	

On another sheet of paper, write a new sentence by scrambling the three parts listed above. For example, use the naming part in #1, the action part in #2, and the where or when part from #3. Draw a picture of your sentence.

Sweet Sentences

Use choices from each part to make three "sweet" sentences.

naming part	action	where or when
I	ate doughnuts	at the bakery
She	ate candy	at the party
He	chewed gum	at the park

Home Sweet Home

Write three sentences about the picture.
For example: The dog is sleeping outside.

1 _____

2 _____

3 _____

The Construction Crew

Write three sentences
about the picture.
Include three parts
in each sentence.

1 _____

2 _____

3 _____

Mystery Boxes

Read the describing words to guess the mystery object. Use the words in the Word Bank.

Describing words help you imagine how something looks, feels, smells, sounds, or tastes. Describing words are called **adjectives**.

Word Bank

ball · bat · silly · blanket · cracker

soft
puffy
warm

I am a _____

I am a _____

hard
wood
long

square
dry
crisp

I am a _____

round
bouncy
red

I am a _____

Sensational Words

Choose words from the Word Bank to describe each picture.

It tastes _____.

It looks _____.

It feels _____.

It feels _____.

It tastes _____.

It sounds _____.

It looks _____.

It sounds _____.

It feels _____.

Word Bank

bumpy

crunchy

furry

gray

red

salty

smooth

squeaky

sweet

Find two objects outside. On another sheet of paper, write two adjectives to describe each object.

More Describing Words

How would you describe a lollipop or a baby chick? Complete the chart below with describing words for each. Choose words from the Word Bank.

Word Bank

thin	thick	smooth	bumpy	fuzzy
soft	hard	fluffy	shiny	sticky

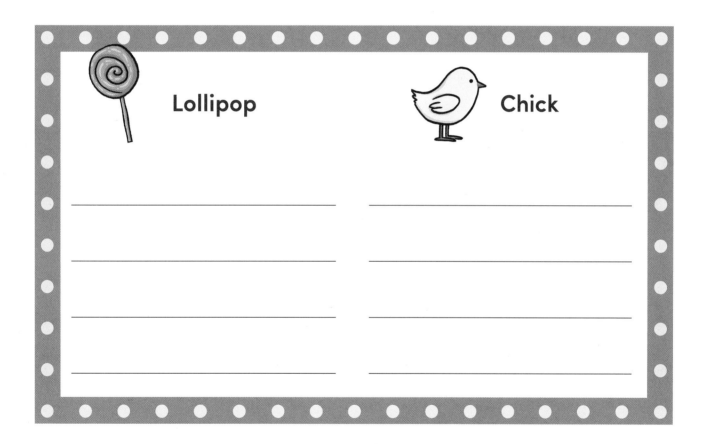

Lollipop

Chick

_____   _____

_____   _____

_____   _____

_____   _____

1 Name something that is thin. _____

2 Name something that is thick. _____

3 Name something that is bumpy. _____

Pretty Packages

Write three words to describe each gift.
Then color them to match.

The describing words
in a sentence help the
reader paint a picture
in his or her mind.

_____ (color)

_____ (color)

_____ (pattern)

_____ (color)

_____ (color)

_____ (pattern)

_____ (color)

_____ (color)

_____ (pattern)

_____ (color)

_____ (color)

_____ (pattern)

What's Inside?

Use describing words to write a sentence about each package.
For example: I found a swimsuit in the **red and yellow** package.

1 I found _____ in the
_____ package.

2 I found _____ in the
_____ package.

3 I found _____ in the
_____ package.

4 I found _____ in the
_____ package.

Around Town

Write a sentence for each picture. Use the describing word in the sentence.

large

beautiful

crowded

noisy

Keep It in Order

Finish each story by writing sentences about the last two pictures.

Sentences can be written in order to tell a story.

First, the spider crawls up.

Next,

Last,

First, there is a tadpole.

Next,

Last,

What's Next?

Finish each set of directions by writing sentences about the last two pictures.

Sentences can be written in order to give directions.

First, mix all the ingredients.

Next,

Last,

First, put your dog in the tub.

Next,

Last,

Which Title Fits?

Match each title with its story.
Write the title above the picture.

The name of a story is called the **title**. It matches with the story. Most of the words in a title begin with capital letters.

A Big Beak	The Big Win
My Space Friend	A Knight's Tale

(title)
_____

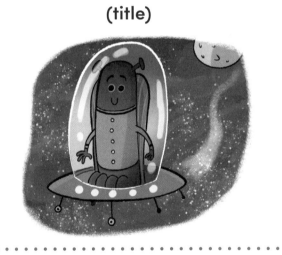

(title)
_____

(title)
_____

(title)
_____

A Terrific Title

Fill in the missing words to make your own story. Then write a title that fits with your story. Draw a picture about your story in the box.

_____

(title)

One _____ day,

_____ took his pet

_____ for a walk. First,

they went to the _____.

Then they walked to _____'s

house. Last, they went home to _____

_____. It was a

_____ day!

Story Strips

> A story has
> a beginning,
> middle, and end.

Write a sentence to tell about each part of the
story. Remember to give the story a title.

Beginning _____
(title)

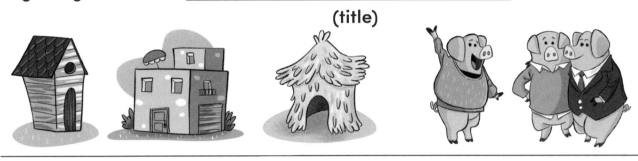

_____
- -
_____

Middle

_____
- -
_____

End

_____
- -
_____

More Story Strips

Think of a story you know well. Write about the beginning, middle, and end parts. Draw pictures to match. Be sure to give your story a title.

_____
(title)

Beginning

Middle

End

ANSWER KEY

Page 5

The	For	That	with	know	but
here	on	When	Have	next	we
as	after	good	Make	there	see
Go	Look	Are	Could	is	why
This	who	said	in	come	them
Has	Name	Before	Her	Where	The

Page 6
1. My dog **2.** She must
3. Maybe she
4. Sometimes she **5.** I think

Page 7
There should be a period at
the end of each sentence.

Page 8
There should be a period at the
end of each sentence.

Page 9
1. Frogs and toads lay eggs.
2. The eggs are in the water.
3. Tadpoles hatch from the eggs.
4. The tadpoles grow legs.
5. The tadpoles lose their tails.

Page 10
1. Tadpoles become frogs
or toads.
2. Frogs live near water.
3. Toads mostly live on dry land.
4. Frogs have wet skin.
5. Toads have bumpy skin.

Page 11
The following sentences
should be colored green:
This is a rug.
The rug has stripes.
Some stripes are green.
Some stripes are yellow.
The rug has a fringe.
The fringe is purple and blue.
The rug is colorful.
The rest are not sentences and
should be yellow.

Page 12

Page 13
Four fish are swimming.
We have one shovel.

Page 14
1. A jaguar is hiding.
2. Some butterflies are blue.
3. Frogs jump in the water.
4. Green snakes hang from trees.
5. The trees grow very tall.

Page 15
The snakes on the left side of the
page should have been colored.

Page 16
1. The blue snakes
2. The yellow snake
3. The green snake
4. The brown snake
5. The red snake
6. The purple snake
7. The black snake
8. The orange snake
Check child's coloring.

Page 17
1. Billy fell on the ice.
2. Cam ran in the race.
3. Ade went inside a dark cave.
4. Dario climbed the hill.
5. Luca swam across the pool.

Page 18
Sentences will vary.

Page 19
Sentences will vary.

Page 20
Sentences will vary.

Page 21
The bones on the right side of
the page should have been
colored.

Page 22
1. is jumping.
2. is playing.
3. is eating.
4. is sleeping.

Page 23
Sentences will vary.

Page 24
1. am **2.** are/were **3.** is/was
4. gets **5.** was **6.** are/were

Page 25
Sentences will vary.

Page 26
Sentences will vary.

Page 27
Drawings will vary.

Page 28
1. long ago 2. yesterday
3. in winter 4. today
5. in the fall 6. last night
7. all day 8. at noon
9. yesterday
10. on Thanksgiving Day
11. this morning 12. Tomorrow

Page 29
Sentences will vary.

Page 30
Sentences will vary.

Page 31
Answers will vary.

Page 32
Sentences will vary.

Page 33
Sentences will vary.

Page 34
Sentences will vary.

Page 35
blanket, bat, cracker, ball

Page 36
sweet, red, smooth
bumpy, salty, crunchy
gray, squeaky, furry

Page 37
Lollipop: hard, shiny, sticky
Chick: soft, fluffy, fuzzy
Answers will vary.

Page 38
Adjectives will vary.

Page 39
Sentences will vary.

Page 40
Sentences will vary.

Page 41
Sentences will vary.

Page 42
Sentences will vary.

Page 43
My Space Friend, A Big Beak
The Big Win, A Knight's Tale

Page 44
Stories will vary.

Page 45
Sentences will vary.

Page 46
Sentences and pictures will vary.